TIME TRAVELING TO
1945

CELEBRATING A SPECIAL YEAR

TIME TRAVELING TO 1945

Author

Clark P. Ridley

Design

Gonçalo Sousa

December 2024

ISBN: 9798303879881

All Rights Reserved

© 2024 Clark P. Ridley

All the images of this book are reproduced under these permissions:

Owner's Permission

Creative Commons License

Fair Use Terms

Public Domain

All images are the property of their respective owners and are protected under international copyright laws.

Surprise!

Dear reader, thank you so much for purchasing my book!

To make this book more (much more!) affordable, the images are all black & white, but I've created a special gift for you!

You can now have access, for FREE, to the PDF version of this book with the original images!

Keep in mind that some are originally black and white, but some are colored.

Go to page 105 and follow the instructions to download it.

I hope you enjoy it!

Contents

Chapter I: News & Current Events 1945

Leading Events	9
Other Major Events	16
Political Events	21
Other Notable Events	25

Chapter II: Crime & Punishment 1945

Major Crime Events	31

Chapter III: Entertainment 1945

Silver Screen	35
Top of the Charts	44
Radio	49

Chapter IV: Sports Review 1945

American Sports	55
British Sports	58
International Sports	61

Chapter V: General 1945

Pop Culture	65
Technological Advancements	69
Fashion	74

Cars	78
Popular Recreation	82

Chapter VI: Births & Deaths 1945

Births	89
Deaths	91

Chapter VII: Statistics 1945 — 93

Cost Of Things	95

Chapter VIII: Iconic Advertisements of 1945 — 97

Chapter I: News & Current Events 1945

Leading Events

Franklin D. Roosevelt Dies - April 12

Franklin D. Roosevelt

The sudden passing of Franklin D. Roosevelt, America's longest-serving president, sent shockwaves through the nation and the world. Leading the country through the Great Depression and most of World War II, Roosevelt was a beacon of resilience, optimism, and innovation. His New Deal policies reshaped the American economy and laid the groundwork for a more robust federal government, while his wartime leadership solidified the US as a global superpower. Despite battling a debilitating illness, Roosevelt remained a master of public connection, inspiring millions through his fireside chats and relentless determination. Vice President Harry S. Truman, relatively new to Roosevelt's inner circle, was thrust into the presidency at a critical juncture. As war raged in Europe and the Pacific, Truman inherited monumental challenges, including the eventual conclusion of World War II and decisions regarding post-war diplomacy.

Roosevelt's death marked the end of an era defined by transformative leadership, but his legacy of bold experimentation and global vision endured. Tributes poured in from across the globe, with many world leaders acknowledging his pivotal role in shaping the Allied victory and the post-war world. While his absence was deeply felt, Roosevelt's influence would continue to shape the course of history for decades to come.

Roosevelt's funeral procession passes through Constitution Avenue

Germany Surrenders: VE Day Celebrated - May 8

Field Marshal Wilhelm Keitel signs Germany's surrender in Berlin

As news of Germany's unconditional surrender spread, jubilation erupted across the Allied nations, marking the end of the war in Europe. Crowds filled the streets of London, Paris, New York, and Moscow, celebrating with parades, music, and spontaneous gatherings. In London, King George VI, Queen Elizabeth, and Winston Churchill appeared on Buckingham Palace's balcony to greet a sea of cheering citizens, while Princess Elizabeth and Princess Margaret mingled incognito with revelers, experiencing the joy firsthand.

Crowds gather outside US and British Embassies in Lisbon on VE Day

In the United States, the occasion coincided with President Truman's birthday, a bittersweet moment as he dedicated the victory to Franklin D. Roosevelt, who had passed away just weeks earlier. Meanwhile, Churchill tempered the celebrations by reminding the world that the war against Japan was still ongoing. Though the mood was festive, the scars of war were visible everywhere, and in places like French Algeria, violent clashes overshadowed the joy. For millions, the

Churchill joins the royal family on Buckingham Palace balcony on VE Day

surrender symbolized relief and a step toward rebuilding shattered lives, but the complexities of post-war politics loomed.

This moment, now celebrated as Victory in Europe Day, remains a symbol of hope, resilience, and the extraordinary relief of peace after years of unimaginable conflict. It was a turning point that redefined nations and set the stage for a vastly changed world order.

Trinity Nuclear Test Conducted - July 16

At a quiet desert site in New Mexico, an event unfolded that would forever alter the course of history: the detonation of the world's first nuclear weapon. Code-named "Trinity," this groundbreaking test marked the culmination of the Manhattan Project's intense efforts. Scientists, led by Robert Oppenheimer, had crafted "The Gadget," an implosion-design plutonium bomb that released a force equivalent to 25 kilotons of TNT. The experiment, conducted in the early hours, illuminated the surrounding mountains like daylight and sent shockwaves felt over 100 miles away.

The "Trinity" nuclear test explosion

The test site, named by Oppenheimer after a John Donne poem, bore witness to awe and unease among the observers. Some marveled at the

Norris Bradbury with the bomb atop the test tower

scientific triumph, while others grappled with its terrifying implications. Oppenheimer himself recalled words from the "Bhagavad Gita": "Now I am become Death, the destroyer of worlds."

Though the test was deemed a success, it left lingering questions about the future of warfare and humanity's relationship with technology. The aftermath saw the creation of trinitite, a radioactive glass, and fallout affecting areas miles away. Trinity was not just a test but a harbinger, unveiling a new, sobering era where human ingenuity and destruction became inseparably intertwined.

Atomic Bomb Developed and Deployed - August 6 & 9

Smoke rises over Hiroshima (left); Nagasaki's atomic bombing (right)

1945

In a war-torn world gasping for resolution, humanity witnessed an event that reshaped history and ethics forever. The detonation of atomic bombs over Hiroshima first, followed by Nagasaki, marked the only use of nuclear weapons in conflict, unleashing devastation so profound it stunned the globe.

Destroyed fire trucks in Hiroshima's wreckage

The loss of life was catastrophic, with tens of thousands killed instantly by the intense heat and shockwaves, while countless others succumbed to burns, radiation sickness, and injuries in the days and months that followed. The bombs not only obliterated infrastructure but left survivors grappling with lifelong trauma and lingering health effects.

In a desperate bid to avoid a protracted and bloody invasion, the Allied forces wielded their most secretive and powerful weapon, targeting cities of military and industrial significance. Japan, reeling from the twin bombings and a Soviet offensive, surrendered just days later, bringing an abrupt end to World War II. This spared millions from further carnage but ignited fierce debates that still persist. Was the decision a tragic necessity to save lives, or an act of disproportionate force that set a chilling precedent? The bombings reshaped global politics, spurring a nuclear arms race and forever altering humanity's approach to warfare, morality, and peace.

End of World War II (Formal Surrender) - September 2

Aboard the USS "Missouri", history witnessed a solemn yet triumphant moment as Japan signed the unconditional surrender, marking the end of the deadliest conflict in human history. The ceremony, meticulously planned

Japanese Minister Mamoru Shigemitsu signs surrender aboard USS Missouri

and attended by Allied leaders, symbolized the culmination of years of global turmoil. The Japanese delegation, led by Foreign Minister Mamoru Shigemitsu and General Yoshijiro Umezu, stood under the weight of their nation's defeat as they signed the instruments of surrender.

The surrender followed a sequence of devastating events: a relentless Allied bombing campaign, the use of two atomic bombs, and a Soviet offensive in Manchuria. Japan, its military incapacitated and economy shattered, faced an ultimatum it could no longer defy. Emperor Hirohito, breaking centuries of imperial tradition, addressed his people, urging them to "endure the unendurable" to secure peace.

As the ink dried on the surrender documents, Allied ships filled Tokyo Bay, and the skies roared with a flyover of hundreds of aircraft, a stark display of military might. The war's official end signaled relief, celebration, and reflection for millions across the globe, yet the complex legacy of the conflict—its destruction, decisions, and aftermath—continues to echo through the pages of history.

Other Major Events

Liberation of Auschwitz & Buchenwald – Jan. 27 & Apr. 11

Soviet soldiers liberate Auschwitz

Amid the grim final months of World War II, two haunting Nazi concentration camps—Auschwitz in occupied Poland and Buchenwald in Germany—were liberated, revealing the horrifying depths of human suffering. At Auschwitz, Soviet forces uncovered thousands of frail survivors alongside mountains of personal belongings and human hair, testaments to the industrial-scale murder of over a million people. Survivors, many too weak to celebrate, found solace in the compassion of their rescuers, who worked tirelessly to provide care amid shock at the atrocities.

Buchenwald survivors return to France

Meanwhile, at Buchenwald, as American troops approached, an audacious SOS from imprisoned resistance fighters helped delay an SS plan to obliterate the evidence. When the U.S. Army arrived, they were greeted by emaciated survivors who, despite their frailty, managed to cheer. American commanders compelled nearby Germans to witness the camp's horrors, ensuring no one could deny the crimes committed there. These liberations became enduring symbols of resilience and humanity's resolve to confront the depths of evil.

Fierce Battle of Manila – Feb. 3 - Mar. 3

US stretcher party carries a wounded soldier through Intramuros ruins

The Battle of Manila unfolded as a harrowing clash of forces, reducing a once-vibrant city to ashes and claiming over 100,000 civilian lives. American and Filipino troops faced fierce resistance from Japanese forces who fortified the city, turning every street and building into a death trap. General MacArthur's drive to liberate the Philippine capital was met with unrelenting brutality from the occupying forces, who committed unspeakable atrocities against the population.

The Japanese Admiral Iwabuchi, determined to defend to the last man, turned Manila into a fiery battleground. While U.S. artillery and ground assaults pushed forward, the destruction of the city's rich architectural heritage was devastating. Iconic sites like Intramuros became symbols of both resilience and ruin.

1945

As liberation finally came, the cost was staggering—historic buildings, cultural treasures, and countless lives lost. This catastrophic chapter remains etched in history, not only as a pivotal moment in the Pacific campaign but as a solemn reminder of war's profound human and cultural toll.

Wounded Japanese forces surrender in Manila

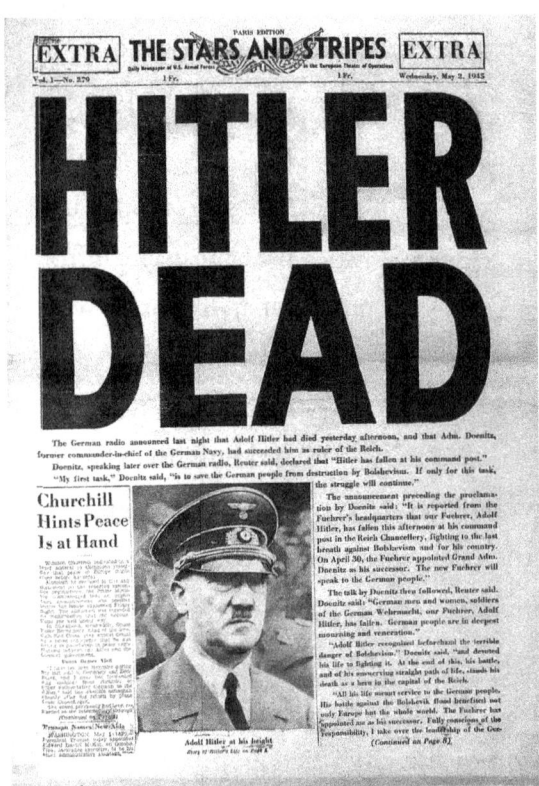

Newspaper "Stars and Stripes" announces Hitler's death

Death of Adolf Hitler - April 30

In the depths of a Berlin bunker, as the Red Army closed in and the Nazi regime crumbled, Adolf Hitler faced the inevitable collapse of his twisted empire. With Eva Braun, whom he had married just hours before, Hitler chose a grim finale, ending his life with a gunshot while Braun succumbed to cyanide. Their bodies were swiftly burned in the Chancellery garden, a final attempt to deny their enemies any grotesque trophies.

This act marked the dismal

conclusion of a tyrant whose policies had unleashed global devastation and unimaginable suffering. News of his death spread swiftly, yet it was shrouded in mystery, thanks to Soviet disinformation campaigns that fueled conspiracy theories for decades. Some whispered that he had escaped to far-flung corners of the world, while others analyzed fragments of evidence to piece together the truth.

Ultimately, Hitler's demise signaled not just the end of a dictator but the implosion of a regime built on hatred and oppression. It was a final chapter in a war that had reshaped history, leaving the world to grapple with its scars and lessons.

Dissolution of the Flensburg Government - May 23

Speer, Dönitz, and Jodl after their arrest

In the shadow of the Third Reich's collapse, the Flensburg Government emerged as a fleeting and desperate attempt to preserve a semblance of Nazi-era authority. Headed by Grand Admiral Karl Dönitz and operating from a naval academy near the Danish border, this interim regime clung to power for mere weeks, claiming governance over fractured and rapidly shrinking territories.

Stripped of diplomatic recognition, ignored by the Allies, and burdened by the weight of Nazi atrocities, the Flensburg administration was little more than a symbolic relic of a defeated state. While Dönitz and his ministers tried to present themselves as a transitional government, their authority was undermined at every turn.

The Allied Powers, initially tolerating the regime to facilitate German military surrender, soon lost patience. British forces stormed the Flensburg headquarters, arresting its members and dissolving the government entirely. This surreal chapter ended with the signing of the Berlin Declaration, erasing the last vestiges of Nazi Germany and paving the way for Allied occupation and reconstruction.

United Nations Founded - October 24

The UN Charter signing on June 26, 1945

Born from the ashes of war and shaped by dreams of lasting peace, the United Nations emerged as a symbol of global unity. The ambitious vision of Franklin D. Roosevelt and his wartime allies, the organization was designed to succeed where the League of Nations had faltered. Crafted through a series of wartime meetings, including the historic Dumbarton Oaks and Yalta Conferences, the framework set the stage for an international body aimed at fostering cooperation, resolving conflicts, and safeguarding human rights.

With the backing of 50 nations, the UN Charter became a bold declaration of shared commitment to a better world. Its formation marked a monumental shift in global governance, placing collective diplomacy at the heart of conflict resolution. The inclusion of a powerful Security Council—

led by the US, UK, Soviet Union, China, and France—promised to balance strength with fairness. The United Nations was more than a peacekeeping mechanism; it was a testament to the power of nations

Leaders of UN member nations during the signing of the UN Charter

uniting for a common purpose, a legacy that endures in its ongoing efforts to tackle global challenges.

Political Events

Yalta Conference Held - February 4-11

Churchill, Roosevelt, and Stalin meet at Yalta to plan postwar Europe

At a picturesque Crimean resort, three towering figures of the 20th century—Roosevelt, Churchill, and Stalin—gathered for a high-stakes chess match over Europe's future. The Yalta Conference was not just a meeting but a pivotal moment where

The Big Three negotiate at Yalta

the Allies plotted the dismantling of Nazi Germany and the reorganization of a war-ravaged continent. Amid grand palaces and diplomatic niceties, Churchill pushed for democracy, Roosevelt sought Soviet support against Japan, and Stalin secured his sphere of influence in Eastern Europe. Promises of free elections clashed with realpolitik as secret deals carved up territories and set the stage for the Cold War.

With every handshake and concession, the leaders sculpted a fragile peace, leaving behind a mix of triumph and trepidation that reshaped the modern world.

Formation of the Arab League - March 22

In Cairo, seven Arab nations came together to form the Arab League, setting the stage for a unified voice in the region. With Egypt, Iraq, Transjordan, Lebanon, Saudi Arabia, Syria, and North Yemen as founding members, the League aimed to strengthen political ties, promote

The Arab League is formed

economic cooperation, and protect the sovereignty of its members. It also sought to address shared cultural, social, and diplomatic challenges, offering a platform for collaboration.

The League's creation was a bold step toward fostering Arab unity, though its history would reveal struggles to achieve deeper integration. Its early actions, such as opposing the partition of Palestine, highlighted the challenges of aligning diverse national interests under one banner. Despite its mixed success, the Arab League remains a vital institution, advocating for the collective interests of the Arab world while navigating the complexities of modern geopolitics.

Churchill Defeated in UK Election - July 5

In a political upset that reshaped Britain's postwar landscape, Winston Churchill, the iconic wartime leader, was defeated as Clement Attlee's Labour Party surged to a historic landslide victory. Despite Churchill's unparalleled wartime popularity, voters turned to Labour's promise of sweeping social reforms, including a National Health Service, full employment, and robust social security. Their manifesto, "Let Us Face the Future," resonated deeply with a nation eager to rebuild after years of hardship.

The campaign revealed a stark divide between Churchill's larger-than-life wartime persona and public doubts about his party's ability to address domestic challenges. Labour's emphasis on housing,

Churchill campaigns with wife Clementine in Woodford, England

welfare, and fair employment won over a populace wary of returning to the struggles of the 1930s.

With this seismic shift, Attlee ushered in an era of transformative policies that laid the foundation for modern British society, while Churchill, though down, remained determined to return to power.

Potsdam Conference Held - July 17 - August 2

Churchill, Truman, and Stalin meet at Potsdam

At a momentous gathering near Berlin, Truman, Stalin, and Churchill—and later Attlee—met at the Potsdam Conference to shape the postwar world. Germany's future took center stage, with agreements to divide the defeated nation into occupation zones and to enforce demilitarization, democratization, and reparations. Borders shifted as Poland's new western boundary moved to the Oder-Neisse line, while "orderly and humane" expulsions of Germans from Eastern Europe were planned, though the human toll proved immense.

The conference wasn't without intrigue. Truman hinted at the U.S.'s powerful new weapon—without revealing its atomic nature—while Stalin played his cards close, well aware of the secret from prior espionage. Meanwhile, shifting alliances emerged as Clement Attlee replaced Churchill mid-conference, and tensions between East and West quietly simmered. Although the leaders departed with a shared vision of peace, unresolved issues and Soviet expansionism soon turned the cooperative spirit of Potsdam into the early rumblings of the Cold War.

Other Notable Events

Death Marches from Concentration Camps – January

As the war neared its end, the Nazis unleashed the horrific death marches, forcing tens of thousands of emaciated prisoners to trek across frozen landscapes toward camps deeper within Germany.

Death march from Auschwitz

These brutal marches aimed to erase evidence of atrocities, keep prisoners as bargaining tools, and exploit their dwindling strength for forced labor. The largest of these began with the evacuation of Auschwitz, where 56,000 prisoners, weakened by starvation and abuse, were marched for miles in deadly winter conditions. Thousands perished along the way.

Those who survived faced further torment: crammed into train cars without food or water, only to be marched again. Entire villages were scarred by mass graves, dug for those who could not endure. These death marches remain a chilling testament to Nazi inhumanity, with stories of survival underscoring both the depth of suffering and the resilience of the human spirit.

Operation Varsity Airborne Assault – March 24

Operation Varsity showcased the Allies' boldness and precision as they executed the largest single-day airborne assault in history. Over 16,000 paratroopers from British and American divisions descended on German soil, accompanied by an impressive fleet of over 1,500 aircraft. The goal: to secure key positions east of the Rhine River and disrupt German defenses, clearing the way for advancing ground forces in Operation Plunder. Despite challenging conditions and pilot errors that misplaced some troops, the operation met its objectives with remarkable speed.

C-47 planes drop paratroopers over the Rhine

Allied forces captured vital bridges, villages, and the strategic Diersfordter Forest, cutting off German reinforcements. Though costly—both divisions suffered over 2,700 casualties—the assault claimed 3,500 German prisoners and shattered enemy morale. Varsity not only cemented Allied dominance but also marked the final significant airborne operation of the war, paving the path to Germany's defeat.

Wesel lies in ruins after Allied bombardment

Victory Parade in Moscow's Red Square - June 24

Moscow's Victory Parade reviewed by Marshal Zhukov

The Moscow Victory Parade on Red Square was a grand spectacle celebrating the Soviet triumph over Nazi Germany. With 40,000 soldiers and 1,850 military vehicles marching under rainy skies, it became the largest and longest military parade in the square's history. The event was meticulously planned, featuring troops from all Soviet fronts, including representatives from the Polish Army, and culminating in the dramatic throwing of captured German standards at Lenin's Mausoleum.
Marshal Zhukov, astride a white stallion, inspected the troops, embodying the might and resilience of the Red Army. Accompanied by a 1,300-member military band, the parade's powerful musical backdrop echoed the victory's magnitude. Although weather curtailed parts of the celebration, the procession symbolized Soviet unity and strength, creating a legacy that resonated in the years to come, with traditions honoring the day continuing to inspire.

Liberation of the Philippines – August 15

Gen. Douglas MacArthur wades ashore during the Leyte landings

The liberation of the Philippines was a dramatic and multifaceted campaign that reshaped the Pacific Theater of World War II. Codenamed Operation Musketeer, this massive effort united American, Filipino, Australian, and Mexican forces to expel Japanese occupiers. Beginning with amphibious assaults on Leyte, the campaign unleashed months of intense battles, including the decisive clashes at Luzon and Mindoro. General Douglas MacArthur's iconic return, supported by guerrilla fighters dynamiting enemy supply lines and sabotaging operations, embodied the promise of freedom.

As the campaign pressed forward, Filipino resilience and allied coordination dismantled entrenched Japanese positions, reclaiming cities and forging critical victories. The fight exacted a heavy toll, with over a million Filipino civilians losing their lives, a

US soldiers on Leyte after landing

sobering reminder of war's cost. Ultimately, the campaign paved the way for Japan's surrender, solidifying the Philippines' role as a symbol of allied strength and enduring courage.

First Edition of "Ebony" Magazine Published - November 1

The debut of "Ebony" magazine marked a groundbreaking moment in publishing, offering an empowering and celebratory platform for African-American stories. Founded by John H. Johnson and inspired by the success of "Life" magazine, its first issue sold out its 25,000-copy print run, showcasing the demand for a publication that reflected the vibrancy and achievements of Black communities. With features on entertainers, political figures, and everyday heroes, the magazine balanced addressing racial issues with highlighting triumphs and resilience.

The first issue of "Ebony" magazine

From Harlem to Hollywood, "Ebony" presented a vision of optimism and excellence, aiming to inspire its readers. Over the years, it became a cultural touchstone, chronicling pivotal movements like civil rights while celebrating influential figures. Its legacy as a voice for progress and pride in Black identity began with that first bold issue, paving the way for decades of impactful storytelling.

Chapter II: Crime & Punishment

Major Crime Events

Himmler's Suicide in British Custody - May 23

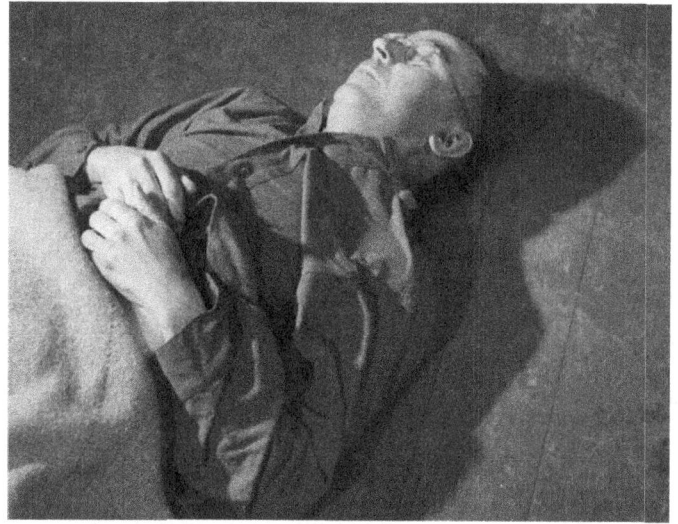

Himmler's body after his suicide in British custody

Heinrich Himmler, one of the most feared architects of the Holocaust, met a swift and ignominious end after his capture by British forces. Disguised as "Sergeant Heinrich Hizinger," Himmler attempted to evade justice in the chaotic final days of the war. His ruse unraveled at a checkpoint when Soviet POWs detained him and noticed inconsistencies in his forged documents. Transferred to British custody, Himmler's identity was soon confirmed. During a routine medical examination, he avoided opening his mouth—until he suddenly bit down on a hidden cyanide capsule. The poison took effect within minutes, ending the life of the man responsible for millions of deaths.
Despite the Allies' efforts to save him for trial, Himmler died before facing justice. His body was buried in an unmarked grave near

Young Heinrich Himmler

Lüneburg, its location forever lost. His death deprived the world of a chance to hold him accountable, leaving only a legacy of horror and infamy.

Pierre Laval Executed for Nazi Collaboration - October 15

Pierre Laval's political trajectory from a leftist lawyer to the prime minister of Nazi-occupied France remains one of history's most controversial. Once a defender of workers, he became infamous for his collaboration with the Nazis, enforcing harsh policies and deporting thousands, including Jews, to their deaths. Laval's actions as head of Vichy France made him a symbol of betrayal in his homeland.

Pierre Laval during his trial

After France's liberation, Laval fled to Spain but returned, was arrested, and faced a tumultuous trial. Believing he could justify his actions as serving France's interests, his defense was overshadowed by a court environment rife with hostility. Found guilty of treason, Laval attempted to evade execution by ingesting poison, but his plan failed. On the morning of his execution, he reportedly shouted, "Vive la France!" before facing the firing squad.
Laval's divisive legacy endures, representing the moral dilemmas and dark compromises of a nation under occupation.

Vidkun Quisling Executed for Treason - October 24

Vidkun Quisling, whose name became synonymous with treachery, faced the ultimate reckoning as justice caught up with Norway's most infamous Nazi collaborator. Once a diplomat and defense minister, Quisling's political

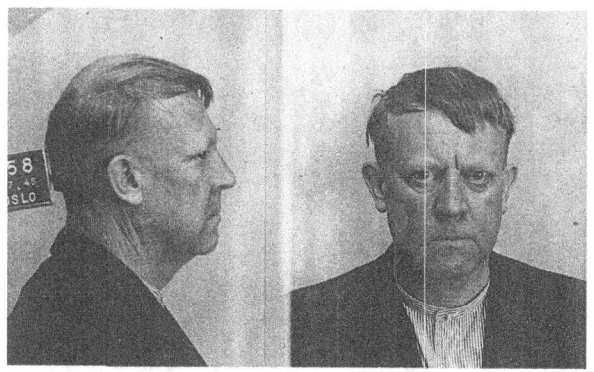

Police photographs Vidkun Quisling

Vidkun Quisling in custody at Akershus Fortress

ambitions took a dark turn when he aligned with Nazi Germany, establishing a puppet government during the occupation. His regime not only supported Nazi war efforts but also enabled the deportation of Norwegian Jews to concentration camps. Captured and tried after the war, Quisling claimed he acted for Norway's benefit, a defense dismissed as hollow by both the court and the public. Found guilty of treason, murder, and embezzlement, he was sentenced to death. His execution at Akershus Fortress symbolized Norway's repudiation of collaboration.

Beyond his death, Quisling's legacy remains one of disgrace. His very name endures in multiple languages as a synonym for betrayal, a stark reminder of the depths to which ambition and allegiance to tyranny can plunge.

Nuremberg Trials Begin - November 20

The Nuremberg Trials marked a pivotal moment in global justice, as the Allies held top Nazi officials accountable for crimes of unprecedented scale. Convened in the ruins of Nuremberg, the trials addressed crimes against peace, war crimes, and crimes against humanity, including the Holocaust's horrors. Twenty-two major leaders stood in the dock, representing the political, military, and economic machinery of Nazi Germany, while additional trials targeted complicit organizations.

Military police guard the courtroom during the first session of the Nuremberg Trials

The proceedings were not only about punishment but also establishing a record of Nazi atrocities and introducing the concept of individual responsibility under international law. Evidence included chilling documents, eyewitness testimonies, and graphic films that laid bare the systematic inhumanity of the regime. Key figures, such as Hermann Göring, were sentenced to death, while others faced lengthy imprisonments.

The trials established new legal precedents, paving the way for modern international criminal law. They also sent a powerful message: no one is above the law, even in the chaos of war.

Chapter III: Entertainment 1945

Silver Screen

The Bells of St. Mary's

Top Film of 1945: The Bells of St. Mary's

When "The Bells of St. Mary's" hit theaters, it delivered a heartfelt blend of comedy, drama, and music that resonated with audiences. Starring Bing Crosby as the easygoing Father O'Malley and Ingrid Bergman as the spirited Sister Benedict, the film spun a tale of resilience and faith as the duo fought to save their dilapidated inner-city school. The story, filled with gentle humor and poignant moments, showcased the unlikely teamwork between the priest and the nun, whose contrasting approaches to life often sparked delightful clashes.

Key to the film's charm was Crosby's relaxed charisma and Bergman's heartfelt performance, earning both actors Academy Award nominations. Crosby even made history as the first actor nominated twice for playing the same character in different films. The movie's success didn't stop there—it became the top-grossing film of its year in the US, solidifying its status as the most profitable film in RKO's history, a major Hollywood studio of the era.

Beyond its box-office triumph, the movie left a cultural imprint, often associated with the Christmas season thanks to its themes of generosity and a memorable Christmas pageant scene. Its legacy has endured, popping up in classics like "It's a Wonderful Life" and "The Godfather". With a mix of laughter, tears, and timeless charm, it remains a cinematic treasure for audiences both then and now.

Remaining Top 3

Mom and Dad

"Mom and Dad" emerged as a cinematic lightning rod, blending controversy, education, and profit in a way few films ever have. Marketed as a "sex hygiene" film, it shocked audiences with its unflinching portrayal of taboo subjects, including premarital sex, pregnancy, and childbirth, complete with graphic medical footage. Directed by William Beaudine and masterminded by Kroger Babb, the film turned provocative content into an educational guise, sidestepping censorship laws while igniting debates across the nation.

Mom and Dad

The story follows Joan Blake, a young woman navigating an unexpected pregnancy after being seduced by a charming pilot. Her struggles expose societal taboos around sex education, culminating in stark lessons on anatomy and responsibility. Despite condemnation from moral watchdogs and countless legal battles—an estimated 428 lawsuits—the film's notoriety fueled its runaway success.

Grossing tens of millions and reaching an audience of over 175 million worldwide, "Mom and Dad" became a cultural phenomenon, solidifying its place in history as the most successful exploitation film ever, with a legacy still debated today.

Leave Her to Heaven

"Leave Her to Heaven" dazzled audiences with its Technicolor allure and darkly captivating tale of obsessive love. Starring Gene Tierney in a career-defining performance, the psychological thriller unfolds as Ellen, a mesmerizing socialite, spirals into jealousy after marrying novelist Richard Harland. Her love, twisted by possessiveness, leads to shocking acts of manipulation, betrayal, and even murder.

Leave Her to Heaven

The film's stunning visuals, juxtaposed with its haunting narrative, elevated it beyond the conventions of film noir and melodrama, blurring genre lines in a way that intrigued critics and audiences alike. Praised for its daring themes and complex characters, Tierney's portrayal earned her an Academy Award nomination, and the film itself won for its breathtaking cinematography.

A box-office sensation, it became Twentieth Century-Fox's highest-grossing film of the decade. Decades later, it retains its cult status, admired for its bold storytelling and chilling exploration of human obsession—a legacy as enduring and unforgettable as Ellen's chillingly destructive love.

Top 1945 Movies at The Domestic Box Office (thenumbers.com)

Rank	Title	Release Date	Gross
1	The Bells of St. Mary's	Dec 7, 1945	$21,300,000
2	Mom and Dad	Jan 3, 1945	$16,000,000
3	Leave Her to Heaven	Dec 20, 1945	$13,800,000
4	The Lost Weekend	Nov 29, 1945	$11,000,000
5	State Fair	Aug 29, 1945	$10,000,000
6	The Dolly Sisters	Oct 5, 1945	$10,000,000
7	The Valley of Decision	May 3, 1945	$9,132,000
8	A Tree Grows in Brooklyn	Feb 28, 1945	$9,000,000
9	Spellbound	Oct 31, 1945	$7,000,000
10	Anchors Aweigh	Jul 19, 1945	$4,600,000

Other Film Releases

In 1945, as the world began to recover from war, cinema offered escapism, hope, and intrigue. Among the mainstream hits, six films stood apart—not for dominating box-office charts, but for their lasting influence and cult status. "Detour", "Dead of Night", "The Picture of Dorian Gray", "And Then There Were None", "The Seventh Veil", and "The Enchanted Cottage" have since transcended their initial receptions, captivating audiences and earning their places as enduring classics.

Leading this selection is Edgar G. Ulmer's "Detour", a quintessential noir hailed for its gritty realism and dark fatalism. Shot with minimal resources, it tells the bleak tale of a pianist who hitchhikes his way into a nightmare of deceit and murder. Its raw, unpolished aesthetic and haunting voiceover encapsulates the despair and paranoia of noir, making it an enduring symbol of the genre's power to explore the human psyche's darker corners.

"Dead of Night", a British anthology horror film, presents a series of eerie supernatural tales, with its story of a ventriloquist's malevolent dummy standing out as particularly chilling. The film's innovative structure and ominous tone influenced the anthology format in horror cinema, establishing it as a touchstone for suspense and psychological terror.

Oscar Wilde's gothic tale of vanity and corruption is brought to life in "The Picture of Dorian Gray". With its striking performances and haunting moral themes, the film explores the consequences of unchecked hedonism and obsession with beauty. Its gothic undertones and unforgettable Technicolor portrait sequence have ensured its place as a psychological thriller and literary adaptation classic.

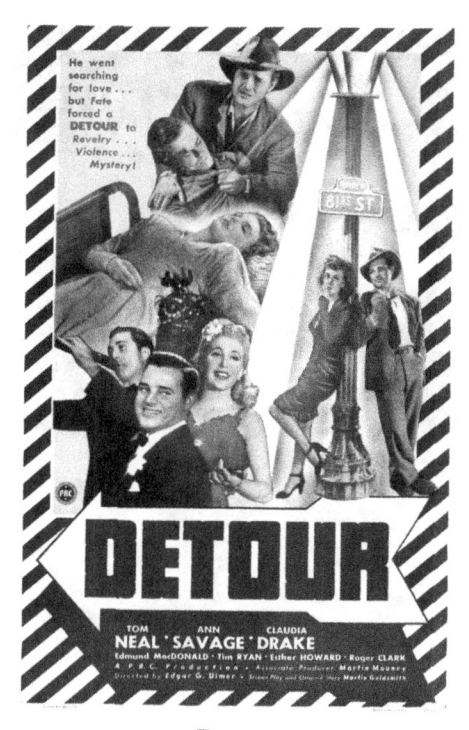

Detour

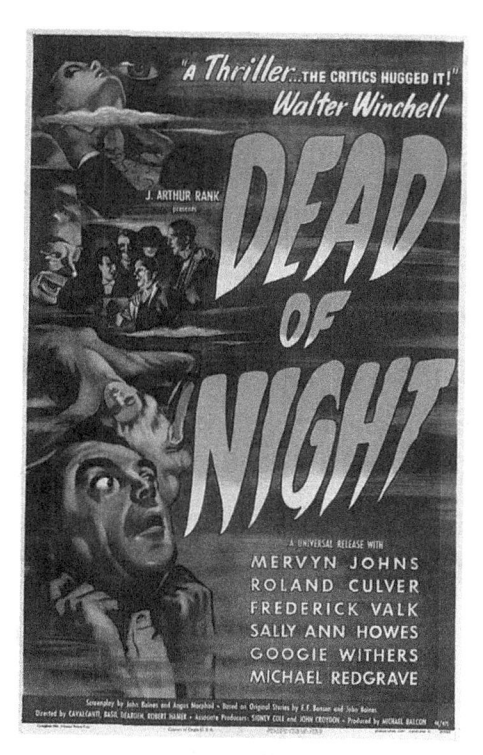

Dead of Night

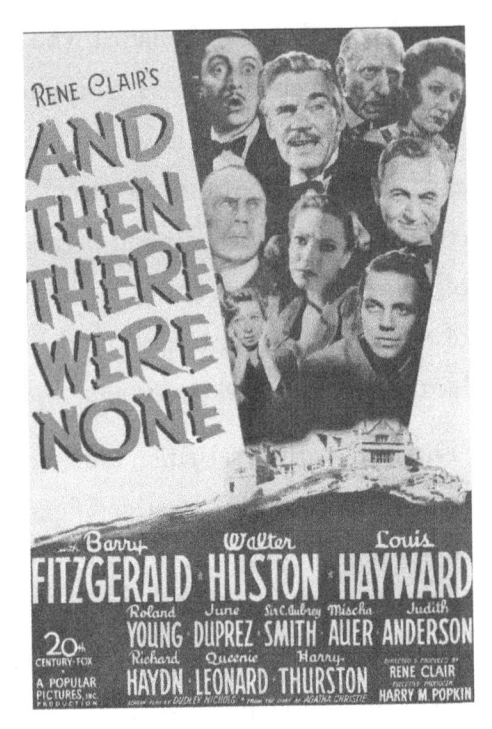

The Picture of Dorian Gray　　　　　　　　　　　And Then There Were None

Agatha Christie's "And Then There Were None" brought the queen of mystery's most famous whodunit to the screen. Ten strangers stranded on a remote island face judgment for their past crimes, with suspense escalating as they are killed one by one. Its tightly woven narrative and intricate character interplay make it a masterpiece of mystery, inspiring countless adaptations and imitations.

"The Seventh Veil" dives into the psychological drama of a troubled concert pianist and her overbearing guardian. Its exploration of trauma, healing, and creative expression, paired with a moving musical score, has kept audiences engaged, making it a standout for its time.

Finally, "The Enchanted Cottage" offers a tender fantasy about love's transformative power. Its heartfelt themes of inner beauty and resilience continue to resonate deeply, maintaining its charm across generations.

Through their innovative storytelling, rich characters, and bold thematic

The Enchanted Cottage

The Seventh Veil

explorations, these films defied their modest box-office beginnings to become timeless pieces of cinematic history, still inspiring audiences and filmmakers today.

The 2nd Golden Globe Awards – Monday, April 16th, 1945

🏆 Winners

Best Performance in a Motion Picture – Actor: Alexander Knox

Best Performance in a Motion Picture – Actress: Ingrid Bergman (Gaslight)

1945

Best Supporting Performance in a Motion Picture – Actor: Barry Fitzgerald (Going My Way)

Best Supporting Performance in a Motion Picture – Actress: Agnes Moorehead (Mrs. Parkington)

Best Director: Leo McCarey (Going My Way)

Best Picture: Going My Way

In 1944, the British Academy Film Awards (nowadays, called the BAFTA Film Awards) did not exist.

The 17th Academy Awards – Thursday, March 15th, 1945 – Grauman's Chinese Theatre, Hollywood, California

🏆 Winners

Best Actor in a Leading Role –
Bing Crosby (Going My Way)

Best Actress in a Leading Role –
Ingrid Bergman (Gaslight)

Best Supporting Actor – Barry Fitzgerald
(Going My Way)

Best Supporting Actress – Ethel Barrymore
(None But the Lonely Heart)

Best Screenplay: Frank Butler and Frank Cavett (Going My Way)

1945

Best Cinematography, Black-and-White:
Joseph LaShelle (Laura)

Best Cinematography, Color:
Leon Shamroy (Wilson)

Best Director:
Leo McCarey (Going My Way)

Best Motion Picture:
Going My Way

Top of the Charts

In 1945, the music scene was characterized by a blend of genres reflecting a world in transition. Swing music, led by big bands, remained popular, providing upbeat rhythms that resonated with audiences. Simultaneously, the emergence of bebop, with pioneers like Charlie Parker and Dizzy Gillespie, introduced complex improvisations that redefined jazz. Country music gained prominence, with artists such as Spade Cooley contributing to the Western swing style. The year also saw the release of notable albums, including Nat King Cole's "King Cole Trio" and Bing Crosby's "Merry

Christmas," which featured the enduring classic "White Christmas." This period laid the groundwork for the diverse musical innovations that would follow in the subsequent decades.

Top Album: "Merry Christmas" by Bing Crosby

Bing Crosby's "Merry Christmas" became a defining holiday album, capturing the spirit of the season and cementing Crosby's status as a cultural icon. Featuring his timeless hit "White Christmas," the best-selling single of all time, the album was an instant success, topping charts for weeks and becoming a perennial favorite. Its warm, nostalgic tone resonated with listeners yearning for comfort during uncertain times. Originally released as a collection of 78 rpm records, the album evolved over the years, with new formats and tracks added, including collaborations with The Andrews Sisters on songs like "Jingle Bells." A re-recording of "White Christmas" in response to worn-out masters only added to its mystique.

Decades later, the album remains a staple of the holiday season, beloved for its enduring charm and a legacy that continues to spread Christmas cheer worldwide.

Merry Christmas

Best Albums and Singles

In 1945, music reflected the complexities of a world in transition, with albums and singles that showcased both artistic innovation and emotional resonance.

1945

Black, Brown and Beige

Strange Fruit

Hot Jazz

On Asch Records

Duke Ellington's "Black, Brown and Beige" offered a sweeping jazz symphony addressing race and culture, while Josh White's "Strange Fruit" delivered haunting social commentary through blues and folk. The Quintet of the Hot Club of France's "Hot Jazz" celebrated gypsy jazz virtuosity, and Coleman Hawkins' "On Asch Records" solidified his legacy as a saxophone pioneer. Champion Jack Dupree brought raw energy to blues piano on "Champion Jack Dupree and His Piano", while Mary Lou Williams explored celestial themes in "Signs of the Zodiac".

Champion Jack Dupree and His Piano

Signs of the Zodiac

🎵 **Top Albums 1945 (besteveralbums.com):**

1. Bing Crosby - Merry Christmas
2. Duke Ellington - Black, Brown And Beige
3. Josh White - Strange Fruit
4. The Quintet Of The Hot Club Of France - Hot Jazz
5. Coleman Hawkins - On Asch Records
6. Champion Jack Dupree - Champion Jack Dupree And His Piano
7. Mary Lou Williams - Signs Of The Zodiac
8. Paul Weston And His Orchestra - Music For Dreaming
9. The Original Broadway Cast - Carousel
10. Wanda Landowska - J.S. Bach: Goldberg Variations

On the singles chart, The Andrews Sisters charmed with their tropical-flavored "Rum & Coca-Cola," and Les Brown's "Sentimental Journey" and "My Dreams Are Getting Better All the Time" captured wartime optimism. Perry Como's "Till the End of Time" brought heartfelt sentiment to the year's music.

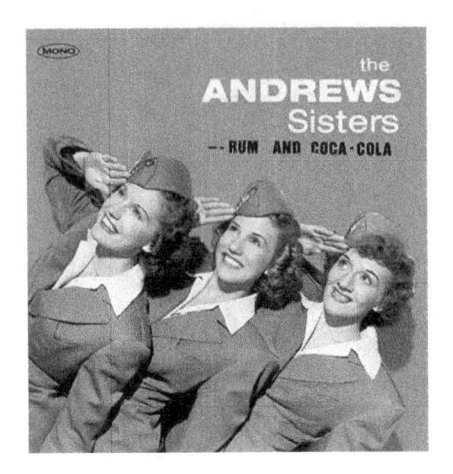

1945

Rum & Coca-Cola

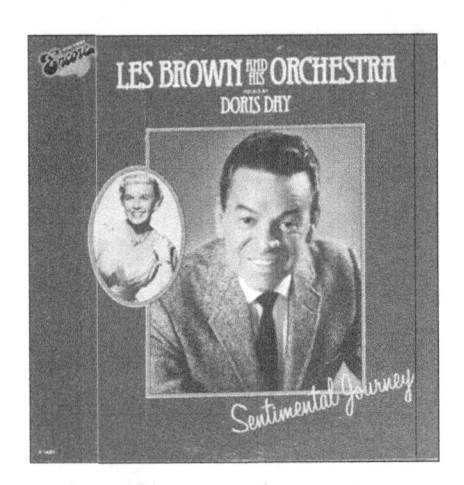

Sentimental Journey

My Dreams Are Getting Better All
the Time

Till the End of Time

🎵 Top Singles 1945 (billboardtop100of.com):

1. The Andrews Sisters – Rum & Coca-Cola
2. Les Brown – Sentimental Journey
3. Perry Como – Till The End of Time
4. Les Brown – My Dreams Are Getting Better All the Time
5. Johnny Mercer – On the Atchison, Topeka & the Santa Fe
6. Harry James – It's Been a Long, Long Time
7. Bing Crosby – I Can't Begin to Tell You

8. Johnny Mercer – Ac-cent-tchu-ate the Positive
9. Sammy Kaye – Chickery Chick
10. Vaughn Monroe – There! I've Said it Again

Award Winners

Neither the Grammy Awards nor the Brit Awards existed in 1945.

Radio

In 1945, radio remained the dominant medium as television was still in its infancy, primarily focused on technological improvements rather than widespread broadcasting. Radio served as the main source of news, entertainment, and morale-boosting content, offering diverse programming including news reports, dramas, and music. It provided essential comfort and connection during the uncertainty of World War II. The era was marked by influential radio broadcasts and popular programs, underscoring radio's vital role as television had not yet become a common or impactful medium in American households. Television began gaining traction after the war, with significant growth in TV sets and stations from 1946 onward, but it wasn't until the late 1940s and early 1950s that TV became a dominant medium in American households.

"The Saint" Premieres on NBC - January 6

"The Saint" leapt from Leslie Charteris's novels to the radio waves, captivating listeners with the adventures of Simon Templar, a charming "Robin Hood"

"The Saint" premieres with Edgar Barrier

who outsmarted both criminals and the law. Premiering with Edgar Barrier in the lead, this swashbuckling series mixed suspense and wit, overseen by its creator to ensure authenticity. With clever scripts and daring escapades, the show's initial run hooked audiences, setting the stage for multiple iterations and a lasting legacy in radio entertainment. A thrilling start for a timeless rogue.

Victory in Europe Celebratory Broadcasts - May 8

As celebratory broadcasts announced Germany's surrender, Churchill and Truman tempered the jubilation with solemn reminders of the ongoing war against Japan. Across Europe and beyond, radios buzzed with messages of triumph, reflection, and resilience. Yet, while many listened in celebration, tragedy struck in French Algeria, where broadcasts coincided with violent massacres during peaceful gatherings. Meanwhile, Austria's Festival of Joy honors these broadcasts, underscoring their historic weight. Victory in Europe resonated through the airwaves, uniting nations in both relief and contemplation.

General Marshall, Fleet Admirals Leahy and King broadcast Victory in Europe from Washington, D.C.

William Joyce's Final Broadcast - April 30

William Joyce, infamously known as Lord Haw-Haw, delivered his final propaganda broadcast as Nazi Germany crumbled. His venomous rhetoric and staunch defiance marked the end of a career built on spreading Nazi ideology through the airwaves. Captured weeks later, Joyce's voice—once a chilling symbol of enemy propaganda—became key evidence in his trial for treason. His broadcasts, once tools of influence, ultimately sealed his fate, as the man who spoke for the Reich met his end under British law's unyielding hand.

William Joyce

Hirohito's Historic Surrender Speech - August 15

Emperor Hirohito in 1935

Hirohito's historic surrender speech

Amid a nation's turmoil, Emperor Hirohito's voice broke centuries of tradition, addressing the Japanese public for the first time via radio. The message, cloaked in formal language and vague phrasing, left many puzzled as it hinted at Japan's surrender. Attempts to sabotage the recording failed, with rebels scouring the palace in vain. Hidden in a lunch bag and lacquer box, the phonograph disks survived, ensuring the Emperor's historic broadcast signaled the end of the war and a call for rebuilding Japan's future.

Iva Toguri, 'Tokyo Rose,' Arrested - September 5

Iva Toguri, mistakenly dubbed "Tokyo Rose," was arrested after Allied forces associated her voice with wartime propaganda broadcasts. Known for her playful remarks and American music on "The Zero Hour", Toguri refused anti-American scripts, even smuggling food to Allied prisoners of war. Despite no clear evidence, public pressure led to her trial and imprisonment. Her broadcasts, aimed at camaraderie rather than propaganda, became a symbol of misjudgment, culminating in her eventual pardon decades later.
A fascinating chapter in wartime radio history.

Iva Toguri, "Tokyo Rose," is interviewed

"Meet the Press" Debuts - October 5

"Meet the Press" made its debut as a groundbreaking radio program, offering a unique platform where influential figures faced direct questioning from journalists. Created by Martha Rountree to promote dialogue and public accountability, the show's first guest was James Farley, a prominent political figure of the New Deal era. This early

Martha Rountree

format, blending tough questions with engaging discussions, set the stage for what would become a cornerstone of American political discourse. Its launch marked the beginning of a legacy in broadcast journalism.

Radio Ratings 1945 (otrcat.com)

1944-45 Radio Programs

Program Title	Network	C.A.B. Rating
Pepsodent Program (Bob Hope)	NBC	34.1
Fibber McGee & Molly	NBC	30.8
Kraft Music Hall (Bing Crosby)	NBC	25.8
The Jergens Journal (Walter Winchell)	NBC	25.3
Mr. District Attorney	NBC	25.1
Lux Radio Theater	CBS	24.5
Chase & Sanborn Program (Edgar Bergen & Charlie McCarthy)	NBC	24.2
Lucky Strike Program (Jack Benny)	NBC	24.2
Sealtest Village Store (Joan Davis)	NBC	24.0
Lady Esther Screen Guild Theater	CBS	23.4

1945-46 Radio Programs

Program Title	Network	C.A.B. Rating
Fibber McGee & Molly	NBC	30.8
Pepsodent Program (Bob Hope)	NBC	29.8
Lux Radio Theater	CBS	27.0

1945

Chase & Sanborn Program (Edgar Bergen & Charlie McCarthy)	NBC	26.9
Raleigh Cigarette Program (Red Skelton)	NBC	25.7
Lucky Strike Program (Jack Benny)	NBC	24.1
Lady Esther Screen Guild Theater	CBS	23.4
Fred Allen Show	NBC	22.7
Mr. District Attorney	NBC	21.1
The Jergens Jounral (Walter Winchell)	Blue	20.3

The Primetime Emmy Awards did not exist in 1945.

Chapter IV: Sports Review 1945

American Sports

Jack Lummus' Heroic Death on Iwo Jima - March 8

From the gridiron to the battlefield, Jack Lummus exemplified heroism in every arena. A former New York Giants player and Baylor sports star, he traded the roar of stadiums for the call of duty in the U.S. Marine Corps. On Iwo Jima, he led his platoon with extraordinary courage, neutralizing enemy strongholds and inspiring his men, even after losing his legs to a landmine. Lying gravely wounded, his final words reflected his unyielding spirit: "The New York Giants lost a good man today." Awarded the Medal of Honor posthumously, Lummus' legacy endures as a symbol of sacrifice, etched in the hearts of Marines and honored by his alma mater.

Jack Lummus

Return of Major League Baseball Post-WWII - April 17

As the crack of the bat returned to stadiums, Major League Baseball roared back post-war, with 16 teams igniting Opening Day

Detroit Tigers in 1945, World Series Champions

excitement. The season culminated in a dramatic World Series clash between the Detroit Tigers and Chicago Cubs, where the Tigers edged out a Game 7 victory. Fans witnessed Hal Newhouser's historic pitching brilliance, clinching a Triple Crown and MVP honors, while Phil Cavarretta's stellar .355 batting average earned him the National League MVP. Yet, travel restrictions still loomed, canceling the All-Star Game. For the Cubs, this marked the end of an era, as they wouldn't see another World Series until over seven decades later.

Byron Nelson Secures PGA Championship – July 15

Byron Nelson's brilliance lit up the fairways as he claimed the PGA Championship at Moraine Country Club, marking his fifth major title and ninth victory in an unprecedented streak of 11 consecutive wins. Facing Sam Byrd, a former pro baseball player, Nelson's precision and dominance secured a 4 and 3 victory in the final match. This wartime championship stood alone as golf's premier event, with Nelson's victory showcasing his unmatched mastery of match play. His triumph not only capped a stellar season but also reinforced his place among golf's greatest legends, blending elegance with resilience during a time when the sport symbolized perseverance and hope.

Byron Nelson at the Miami International Four-Ball Tournament

US Open Tennis Championships Held - September 1945

The U.S. National Championships brought tennis back to center stage, offering a thrilling showcase of skill and resilience. On the grass courts of Forest Hills, Frank Parker triumphed in a grueling men's singles final, while

1945

The 1945 US Open Tennis Championships

Sarah Palfrey Cooke staged a stunning comeback to claim the women's title. Doubles matches delivered edge-of-your-seat excitement, with Gardnar Mulloy and Bill Talbert clinching a marathon victory in men's doubles. Louise Brough and Margaret Osborne dominated women's doubles, and Osborne joined Talbert again to secure the mixed doubles crown. As the sole Grand Slam of the year due to wartime, this tournament symbolized the enduring spirit of sport amid global challenges.

Frank Parker

Sarah Cooke

Cleveland Buckeyes Win Negro World Series – September 20

The Cleveland Buckeyes dominated the Negro World Series, sweeping the powerhouse Homestead Grays in a stunning four-game showcase of grit and precision. Behind lights-out pitching and clutch hitting, the Buckeyes silenced the Grays' bats, with Frank Carswell sealing the series with a brilliant shutout in the finale. Standout performances from Willie Grace and Quincy Trouppe highlighted Cleveland's offense, while their defense proved unyielding. This victory marked a crowning achievement for the Buckeyes, toppling the perennial champions and cementing their place in baseball history. As fans packed stadiums from Cleveland to Philadelphia, the series embodied the resilience and skill of the Negro Leagues during a transformative era for the sport.

The 1945 Cleveland Buckeyes
The winning team

British Sports

Red Rower Captures Cheltenham Gold Cup – March 17

In a dazzling display of resilience and skill, Red Rower, an eleven-year-old veteran of the racetrack, triumphed in the Cheltenham Gold Cup amidst a record field of sixteen competitors. Once considered an underdog, Red Rower's journey to glory was marked by near misses and wartime interruptions. After early promise and heartbreakingly close finishes in previous Gold Cups, he returned to a festival reshaped by wartime restrictions, proving his mettle on the grand stage. Guided by jockey Davy

Jones, he held steady with the leaders before seizing the advantage at the final fence, powering home to victory. This crowning achievement highlighted not just the determination of a remarkable horse but also the enduring spirit of National Hunt racing during turbulent times.

Red Rower guided by jockey Davy Jones

Dante Claims Derby Victory – June 9

Dante, a remarkable colt trained in northern England, made history with a dazzling victory in the Derby Stakes. Despite battling a degenerative eye condition that would eventually blind him, he delivered a thrilling performance that left a crowd of 30,000, including the King and Queen, in awe. Starting as the favorite, Dante surged from the back of the pack in the final stretch, outpacing rivals to claim victory by two lengths. His win marked the first Derby triumph for a northern-trained horse since 1869, sparking widespread celebration in Yorkshire.

Dante's career, though tragically cut short by health issues, solidified his legacy. Praised as one of the finest horses of his era, his Derby success remains a symbol of resilience and brilliance, inspiring the race named in his honor at York Racecourse.

Dante in Middleham in 1945

Scotland Seizes British Victory Home Championship – 1945-46 Season

England vs Scotland, March 16, 1946

In a post-war celebration of football's revival, Scotland emerged triumphant in the British Victory Home Championship, showcasing dominance over their Home Nation rivals. Unbeaten across three matches, Scotland sealed their victory with key performances, including a decisive win over Wales and a hard-fought triumph against England at Hampden Park. Their campaign was marked by resilience and flair, with players like Billy Liddell and Peter Dodds providing standout moments that electrified the crowds. The tournament, steeped in the joy of renewed peace, was a spirited display of national pride, even as matches were classified as Victory Internationals rather than full-fledged contests. Scotland's success in the championship not only secured their place as champions but also symbolized the enduring power of sport to unite and inspire in challenging times.

Football League Returns in England – September 1945

The return of competitive football in England marked a hopeful chapter as the nation transitioned from wartime to peace. The 1945–46 season, though unconventional, saw the revival of the FA Cup alongside regional competitions, Football League North and South, bridging the gap until the full league program could resume. Clubs from the top two divisions adapted to these temporary formats, with Derby County claiming FA Cup glory in a unique edition featuring two-legged ties up to the quarter-finals. This transitional season symbolized resilience and the unifying power of football.

Sheffield United and Birmingham City topped their respective regional leagues, keeping fans entertained while eagerly anticipating a full return to normalcy. The stage was set for the grand comeback of England's beloved Football League in the following season, rekindling football's timeless spirit.

Derby County, 1944-1945 season

International Sports

Toronto Maple Leafs Dominate Stanley Cup – April 6-22

The Toronto Maple Leafs delivered a thrilling performance to claim the Stanley Cup in a nail-biting seven-game series against the Detroit Red Wings. Starting with three consecutive wins, the Leafs seemed poised for a sweep, with rookie goalie Frank McCool achieving an impressive shutout streak. However, the Red Wings roared back, fueled by Ted Lindsay and Harry Lumley, forcing a dramatic Game 7 after back-to-back shutouts. The decisive game saw Babe Pratt score the winning goal in

Toronto Maple Leafs win the 1945 Stanley Cup

a tense 2–1 victory, cementing the Leafs' triumph and narrowly avoiding a historic comeback by Detroit. The series marked the first finals where both teams started rookie goaltenders, showcasing the future stars of hockey. This hard-fought victory not only demonstrated Toronto's resilience but also left an indelible mark on Stanley Cup history, embodying the fierce rivalry and passion of the sport.

John A. Kelley Reclaims Boston Marathon Glory - April 16

John A. Kelley, a legendary figure in long-distance running, reclaimed his place in history with a stunning victory at the Boston Marathon, ten years after his first triumph.

Johnny Kelley finishes the Boston Marathon

Known as "Kelley the Elder," he battled the grueling Massachusetts course with precision and grit, outpacing the competition to secure his second title. Kelley's win was a testament to endurance and determination, as he competed in his 17th Boston Marathon amidst a field of elite athletes. Celebrated for his longevity, Kelley would go on to participate in the marathon over 60 times, cementing his reputation as a cornerstone of the event's history. His victory in this iconic race not only showcased his remarkable talent but also inspired generations of runners who continue to aspire to his legendary status. Kelley's name remains synonymous with the spirit and tradition of the Boston Marathon.

Hoop Jr. Wins Kentucky Derby – June 9

Hoop Jr. wins the Kentucky Derby with Eddie Arcaro

In a Kentucky Derby like no other, Hoop Jr., under the skilled guidance of jockey Eddie Arcaro, galloped to victory in an extraordinary race shaped by wartime disruptions. Initially postponed from its traditional May slot due to a government suspension on horse racing, the event was rescheduled shortly after V-E Day, making it a triumphant return for the sport and its fans. Hoop Jr., trained by Ivan H. Parke and owned by Fred W. Hooper, crossed the finish line in 2:07, defeating rivals Pot O'Luck and Darby Dieppe. This Derby became a symbol of resilience, with its late timing and altered stakes lineup reflecting the tenacity of an industry adapting to global upheaval. Hoop Jr.'s win not only crowned a remarkable performance but also celebrated the enduring spirit of competition and tradition during challenging times.

Horses at the first turn of the Kentucky Derby

East Fremantle Claims WANFL Premiership - October 13

East Fremantle dominated the 1945 WANFL season, capping it with a resounding victory in the Grand Final against South Fremantle at Subiaco Oval. Overcoming a fiercely competitive field, East Fremantle's precision and depth were unmatched, leading them to a 12.15 (87) to 7.9 (51) win. The match saw a standout performance from Alan Ebbs, who earned the inaugural Simpson Medal for best on ground, cementing his place in history.

George Doig

This victory marked a triumphant return to open-age competition after wartime restrictions, with East Fremantle reclaiming their dominance from previous seasons. Their cohesive teamwork, highlighted by key contributions from players like Meiers and George Doig, was too much for a determined but outclassed South Fremantle. Celebrated by a crowd of 21,000 fans, East Fremantle's victory added another illustrious chapter to their storied legacy in Western Australian football.

A long tradition: the team in 1925

Chapter V: General 1945

Pop Culture

"Anchors Aweigh" Released in Theaters - July 19

Two sailors, a shy crooner and a charming dancer, embark on a lively Hollywood adventure in "Anchors Aweigh". This Technicolor musical dazzles with Gene Kelly's iconic duet with animated Jerry Mouse, Frank Sinatra's heartfelt ballads, and a heartfelt quest to help an aspiring singer. Featuring lavish sets, toe-tapping numbers, and a patriotic finale, the film became a box office triumph and an Oscar winner for its memorable score. A delightful blend of romance, humor, and show-stopping performances, it remains a cinematic classic.

Anchors Aweigh

"Mildred Pierce" Hits Theaters - September 28

Joan Crawford shines in "Mildred Pierce", a gripping mix of melodrama and noir that explores ambition, sacrifice, and betrayal. As a mother striving to please her ungrateful daughter, Crawford

Mildred Pierce

delivers an Oscar-winning performance in a tale of love turned toxic. Directed by Michael Curtiz, the film dazzles with shadowy cinematography and complex characters, including Ann Blyth as the venomous Veda. With twists, murder, and sharp dialogue, this classic captivates as both a cautionary tale and a triumph of Crawford's talent.

First Ballpoint Pen Hits New York Shelves - October 29

The ballpoint pen revolutionized writing when it hit store shelves, promising a sleek, smudge-free alternative to fountain pens. The "Reynolds Rocket" debuted at a New York department store, dazzling shoppers despite its hefty $12.50 price tag. Designed with innovative ball-and-ink technology, it marked the beginning of a new era for writing instruments. Thousands rushed to buy this modern marvel, transforming a once niche invention into an everyday essential, paving the way for today's global ballpoint dominance.

Laszlo Biro invents the ballpoint pen

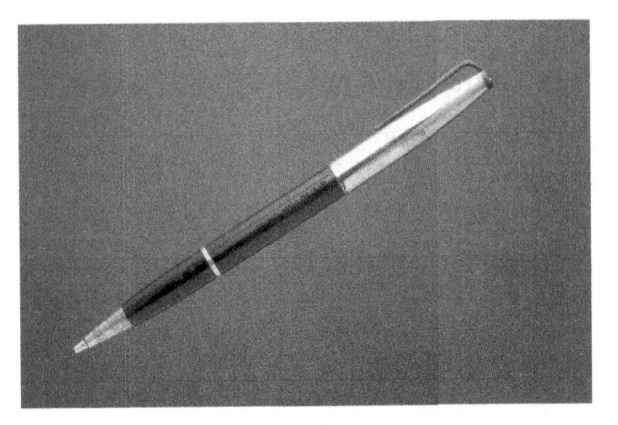

Early ballpoint pen from 1945

Hitchcock's "Spellbound" Premieres - October 31

Alfred Hitchcock's "Spellbound" mesmerized audiences with its gripping tale of love, mystery, and psychological intrigue. Ingrid Bergman and

Gregory Peck shine as a psychoanalyst and an amnesiac entangled in a web of murder and hidden memories. Featuring Miklós Rózsa's Oscar-winning score and Salvador Dalí's surreal dream sequences, the film blended suspense and

Spellbound

art in groundbreaking ways. A box-office triumph and critical darling, it cemented Hitchcock's status as the master of suspense, captivating viewers with its haunting exploration of the human mind.

Slinky Toy Makes Its Debut – November

The debut of the metal Slinky toy

The Slinky made a playful splash in toy history with its dazzling debut at Gimbels in Philadelphia, selling out 400 units in just 90 minutes. Created by naval engineer Richard T. James after witnessing a spring "walk" off a shelf, the coil's mesmerizing motion turned a simple idea into a phenomenon. Priced at $1, it wasn't just a toy—it became a tool for science classes, a wartime radio antenna, and even a NASA experiment in zero gravity. With its gravity-defying tricks and universal charm, the Slinky cemented its place as a timeless icon of ingenuity and fun.

"The House I Live In" Debuts - December 9

Frank Sinatra took a stand against prejudice in "The House I Live In", a powerful ten-minute short film promoting tolerance and unity. Playing himself, Sinatra interrupts a group of boys harassing another child and delivers a heartfelt speech about equality, emphasizing that everyone is an American, regardless of background. Featuring the poignant title song, the film struck a chord with audiences and earned both an Honorary Oscar and a Golden Globe. Its timeless message and Sinatra's earnest performance secured its place as a culturally significant classic.

The House I Live In

Most Popular Books from 1945 (goodreads.com)

1. Animal Farm - George Orwell
2. Pippi Longstocking (Pippi Långstrump, #1) - Astrid Lindgren
3. Brideshead Revisited: The Sacred and Profane Memories of Captain Charles Ryder - Evelyn Waugh
4. The Glass Menagerie - Tennessee Williams
5. Cannery Row (Cannery Row, #1) - John Steinbeck
6. Stuart Little - E.B. White
7. A History of Western Philosophy - Bertrand Russell
8. Black Boy - Richard Wright

9. The Aleph and Other Stories - Jorge Luis Borges
10. That Hideous Strength (The Space Trilogy, #3) - C.S. Lewis
11. Ross Poldark (Poldark, #1) - Winston Graham
12. Sparkling Cyanide (Colonel Race, #4) - Agatha Christie
13. The Age of Reason (Roads to Freedom, #1) - Jean-Paul Sartre
14. The Pursuit of Love (Radlett & Montdore, #1) - Nancy Mitford

Technological Advancements

Mass Production of Penicillin Accelerates – February

Thousands of glass fermentation vessels like this one were used in laboratories to produce penicillin

In the midst of the war-torn 1940s, the mass production of penicillin marked a groundbreaking chapter in medical history. Originally discovered by Alexander Fleming in 1928 and refined by Howard Florey's Oxford team a decade later, this "miracle drug" turned the tide in treating bacterial infections. The production leap was driven by collaboration between scientists and industry, with innovative techniques like deep submergence fermentation amplifying yields. By replacing sugar with corn steep liquor, researchers dramatically enhanced efficiency, transforming a laboratory breakthrough into a global lifesaver.

First saving soldiers on the battlefield, penicillin soon became accessible to civilians, ushering in the antibiotic era. Its journey from a moldy laboratory dish to mass production showcases the transformative impact of innovation and determination on humanity's fight against illness.

Worker sprays penicillin mold solution into flasks to encourage further penicillin growth

Von Neumann's EDVAC Report Released - June 30

John von Neumann's First Draft of a Report on the EDVAC (Electronic Discrete Variable Automatic Computer) unveiled a revolutionary vision for computing, introducing the now-iconic stored-program concept. Handwritten during his commutes, the report outlined a system where memory unified instructions and data, powered by vacuum tubes instead of sluggish relays. Its design featured binary numbers, two's complement arithmetic, and logical subdivisions like arithmetic, control, and memory units. While hailed as the foundation of modern computer architecture, the report sparked controversy.

Von Neumann (right) with J. Robert Oppenheimer

Other contributors to the EDVAC project felt overlooked, as von Neumann's role seemed overstated. Despite the drama, the draft inspired a global wave of innovation, forever altering the trajectory of computational design and technology.

The AVIDAC computer (shown in the image) was partially based on the architecture of the Institute for Advance Study machine developed by Von Neumann

Lockheed P-80 Shooting Star: First Operational Jet Fighter – August

The Lockheed P-80 Shooting Star soared into history as America's first operational jet fighter, embodying cutting-edge technology with its sleek, straight-wing design and turbojet engine. Developed in an astonishing 143 days by Lockheed's Skunk Works team, the jet marked a leap forward in air combat capabilities, outpacing piston-driven predecessors and setting the stage for modern fighter aircraft. Although it saw limited service in Italy near the end of World War II, it quickly became a pioneer in jet-powered aviation. Later, the P-80's legacy extended through its role in the Korean War and its evolution into the T-33 trainer, which remained in service for decades, cementing its place in aviation history.

US Air Force Lockheed P-80 Shooting Star

Folic Acid Developed in Pure Crystalline Form - 1945 (Exact Date Unknown)

The development of folic acid in pure crystalline form was a milestone in nutritional science, unlocking powerful applications for health. This synthetic version of vitamin B9, derived from leafy greens, became a vital tool in preventing neural tube defects during pregnancy and treating anemia caused by folate deficiency.

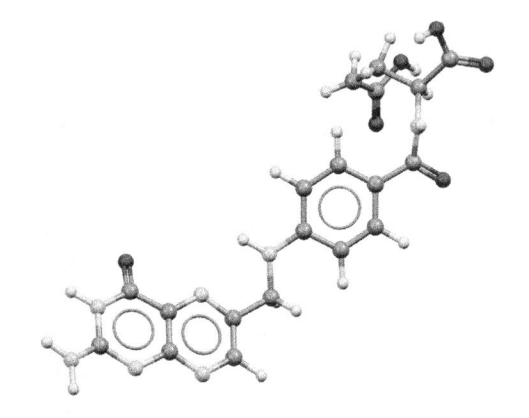

Ball-and-stick model of a folic acid molecule

Its stability made it perfect for food fortification, helping to combat widespread nutrient deficiencies globally. Beyond its role in supporting DNA synthesis and cell division, folic acid also found its way into chemotherapy and cardiovascular health. This breakthrough not only enhanced public health but also set the stage for further exploration into vitamins' roles in preventing disease and promoting well-being, leaving a lasting legacy in medical science.

Pure folic acid powder

Percy Spencer Patents Microwave Oven - October 8

Percy Spencer's accidental discovery revolutionized kitchens worldwide when he found a magnetron's microwaves could heat food—starting with a melted candy bar in his pocket. Experimenting further, he popped popcorn and warmed water, sparking the creation of the first microwave oven, the "Radarange." Initially, this six-foot, 750-pound behemoth was

Percy Spencer

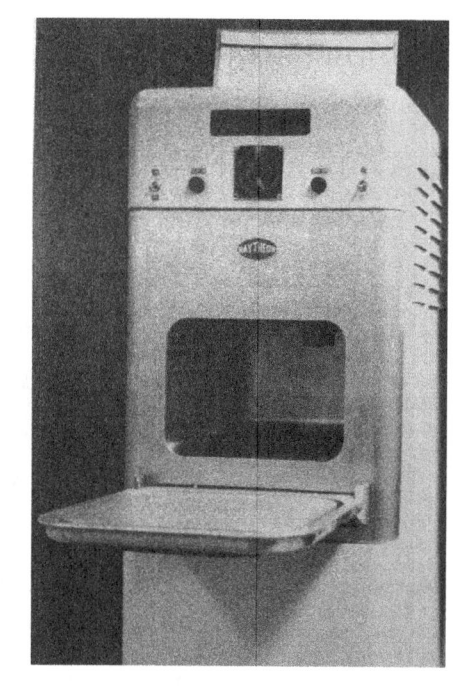

Raytheon model 1132, the first Radarange TM

used commercially, but its hefty price and public wariness delayed its domestic adoption. Decades later, smaller, affordable models like the Amana Radarange brought microwaves into everyday homes, reshaping cooking forever. Spencer, a self-taught genius who rose from humble beginnings to innovate at Raytheon, turned a sweet accident into one of the most transformative inventions in modern kitchen history.

ENIAC Completion Marks a Technological Milestone – November

ENIAC, the world's first programmable electronic computer, marked a leap in technology by performing calculations 1,000 times faster than its electromechanical predecessors. Designed to compute artillery firing tables, it became a marvel of versatility, capable of tackling complex problems like thermonuclear weapon feasibility.

Weighing over 30 tons and powered by 18,000 vacuum tubes, ENIAC's operation required programming via cables and switches—a process that could take weeks. Despite its size and quirks, including frequent tube failures, it showcased unprecedented speed and power. Its completion not only revolutionized computing but also laid the groundwork for modern programmable systems, making it a landmark in technological innovation and a symbol of the dawn of the digital age.

Two pieces of ENIAC currently on display in the Moore School of Engineering and Applied Science

Fashion

In 1945, fashion reflected the dual influence of wartime austerity and the anticipation of post-war renewal. Clothing choices were shaped by material shortages and rationing, leading to designs that prioritized practicality while retaining a sense of elegance and individuality.

Women's attire embodied a utilitarian yet distinctly feminine aesthetic. "Utility" clothing, introduced during the war,

Women's fashion in '45

Men's fashion in '45

Women's "utility" style during wartime

The typical 1945 suits

featured simple lines and minimal embellishments to conserve fabric. Dresses commonly showcased padded shoulders, nipped-in waists, and knee-length A-line skirts, creating a modest hourglass silhouette. Fabrics such as rayon and gabardine became prevalent as silk and wool were scarce. The "shirtwaist" dress, characterized by its button-down front and tailored fit, was widely embraced for its practicality and modest appeal. Separates gained prominence, allowing women to mix and match pieces to extend their wardrobes. High-waisted skirts paired with fitted blouses or knit sweaters were common ensembles. Trousers, which had once been largely reserved for men, gained acceptance among women, particularly those engaged in wartime labor. These trousers often featured wide legs and high waists, combining practicality with a functional style.

Shirtwaist dress

'45 everyday fashion included slacks and button-down shirts

Men's fashion leaned heavily towards conservative and functional styles, reflecting the continued influence of military aesthetics. Suits typically had broad shoulders and straight, roomy trousers. Single-breasted jackets with notched lapels were the norm, often in muted colors such as navy, gray, and brown. Fabric rationing limited decorative details, resulting in streamlined suits devoid of excess pockets or cuffs. Casual attire featured wool sweaters, plaid shirts, and sturdy trousers, while outerwear included military-inspired bomber jackets and trench coats. Accessories remained understated, with narrow ties, functional wristwatches, and hats such as fedoras and flat caps being common.

Accessories reflected the era's resource-conscious ethos. Women favored simple hats like berets or turbans, often crafted from non-traditional materials, and modest jewelry made of non-precious substances. Gloves and practical handbags were common for formal occasions. Footwear, limited by rationing, included sturdy, low-heeled shoes, with soles made from alternatives like cork or wood. Men's accessories followed a similar restraint, with durable

1945

Men's style was mainly conservative and functional

Women loved berets in '45

leather oxford and derby shoes complementing their understated attire. Youth fashion offered subtle variations on adult styles. Girls often wore knee-length skirts paired with tucked-in blouses and accessorized with neckerchiefs. Boys adopted high-waisted trousers with collared shirts and suspenders. The zoot suit, notable for its exaggerated proportions, symbolized youthful rebellion, though its extravagant fabric use made it controversial during a time of scarcity.

Men's grey fedora hat with black band

Fashion in 1945 captured a period of transition, blending wartime necessity with expressions of individuality and hope for the future. This balance between practicality and resourcefulness created enduring styles that laid the groundwork for the more extravagant designs of the post-war era.

Young men pose in zoot suits

Cars

In 1945, the automotive industry began a complex recovery after years of wartime production. Civilian car manufacturing had been largely suspended, with factories repurposed to produce military equipment. As the war concluded, manufacturers gradually shifted back to consumer markets. New models were virtually nonexistent, but pre-war designs were slowly reintroduced. This transitional year reflected the industry's resilience and its determination to rebuild and innovate in the post-war era.

Top Selling Cars

U.S.A

Civilian car production in the United States remained effectively halted in 1945 as factories focused on retooling for peacetime. Pre-war models, including the Chevrolet Fleetmaster and Ford Deluxe, were prepared for reintroduction but would not see substantial production until 1946.

1945 Chevrolet Fleetmaster

1945 Ford Deluxe Convertible

Cars available to Americans in 1945 were largely pre-war vehicles, either maintained throughout the war or acquired secondhand, as pent-up demand for reliable transportation awaited fulfillment.

U. K.

In the United Kingdom, production of civilian vehicles resumed cautiously, with most of the output prioritized for export to aid economic recovery. The Austin Ten, a staple of pre-war Britain, reentered production with few modifications. Its 1.2-liter engine offered efficiency and durability, making it ideal for resource-strapped drivers. Another returning favorite was the Morris Eight, known for its compact size and affordability, well-suited to

1945 Austin Ten

1945 Morris Eight E Staff Car

Britain's constrained post-war resources. These models underscored the necessity of practicality and reliability during this challenging period.

Fastest Car

The Alfa Romeo 6C 2500 Super Sport, originally introduced before the war, remained one of the fastest and most luxurious cars available in 1945. Powered by a 2.5-liter inline-six engine producing 105 horsepower, it reached speeds of 106 mph (170.6 km/h). Its streamlined design by Touring Superleggera blended elegance with aerodynamics, keeping it a symbol of high performance and sophistication during an otherwise subdued year for performance vehicles.

1945 Alfa Romeo 6C 2500 Super Sport

Most Expensive American Cars of 1945

American luxury car production had not resumed in 1945, with manufacturers focusing on returning to mass-market production. Pre-war luxury models such as the Packard Custom Super Eight and Lincoln Zephyr remained coveted symbols of craftsmanship and opulence. These vehicles were often refurbished or preserved by affluent owners, maintaining their

1945 Packard Custom Super Eight

reputation despite the absence of new production. Packard, in particular, exemplified a legacy of luxury that would fully resume post-war.

1945 Lincoln Zephyr

Most Powerful Muscle Car of 1945

1945 Buick Roadmaster

The term "muscle car" had yet to be coined, but performance-oriented vehicles of the time hinted at what was to come. The Buick Roadmaster, reintroduced in limited numbers in 1945, featured a straight-eight engine with ample power for its class. While primarily a luxury vehicle, its solid performance and engineering foreshadowed the evolution of American high-performance cars that would define the 1960s muscle car era.

The year 1945 marked a slow but determined transition for the automotive industry as manufacturers began shifting from military to civilian production. Practical vehicles like the Austin Ten and Morris Eight addressed the immediate needs of British consumers, while the U.S. awaited a resurgence of production from companies like Chevrolet and Ford. High-performance models such as the Alfa Romeo 6C 2500 Super Sport carried on the tradition of excellence in engineering and design, and luxury brands like Packard preserved their legacy despite production halts. These vehicles reflected a resilient industry, balancing post-war recovery with the promise of future innovation and growth.

Popular Recreation

The year 1945 marked a pivotal moment in history as World War II ended, ushering in a transition from wartime austerity to peacetime normalcy. This shift was reflected in the era's recreational activities, which blended wartime influences with renewed enthusiasm for traditional and emerging pastimes.

Glenn Miller and His Orchestra

Music remained central to leisure, serving as both a morale booster and a celebratory outlet. Swing and big band music, led by artists like Glenn Miller and Benny Goodman, set the tone for jubilant dances. However, bebop jazz, pioneered by musicians such as Charlie Parker and Dizzy Gillespie, began influencing music culture with its faster tempos and complex rhythms.

Popular songs like "Sentimental Journey" by Les Brown and Doris Day and "Rum & Coca-Cola" by The Andrews Sisters reflected the optimistic post-war mood. Dance halls remained lively, with ballroom styles like the foxtrot and waltz gaining prominence alongside the jitterbug. In the UK, wartime favorites fostered unity at community dances.

Radio was a cornerstone of entertainment and information. Shows like "The Jack Benny Program" in the US and "ITMA" (It's That Man Again) in the UK attracted millions, offering humor and distraction. By 1945, nearly ten million radio licenses had

Foxtrot in '45

"The Jack and Benny Program"

The British comedian Tommy Handley rehearses with actors from his "ITMA show"

83

Brief Encounter

been issued in Britain, highlighting the medium's importance. Cinema boomed as audiences sought escapism and reflection. Films such as "Brief Encounter" in the UK and "Mildred Pierce" in the US blended romance, drama, and optimism with narratives resonating with wartime and post-war realities.

Sports played a key role in helping societies rebuild and reconnect. Baseball thrived in the US, with returning athletes energizing professional leagues. In the UK, football (soccer) leagues resumed, drawing massive crowds, while cricket brought communities together to celebrate peace. Outdoor activities like hiking, fishing, and picnicking grew in popularity as affordable family pastimes. Cycling became a staple for both transportation and leisure, offering mobility and freedom.

Baseball drew massive crowds in the 1940s

Children's play in 1945 bridged tradition and innovation. The Slinky, introduced that year, became an instant classic. Traditional toys like marbles, jump ropes, and dolls encouraged creativity

1945

Girls jumping rope

Children playing marbles in 1945

A young girl with her doll and tea set

The original 1945 Slinky toy

and physical activity. Boys often played with toy soldiers, reflecting lingering wartime influences, while girls enjoyed dolls and tea sets mirroring domestic life. Meccano sets provided hands-on opportunities to construct mechanical models, fostering technical skills and imagination. Outdoor games like hopscotch and roller skating were enjoyed on both sides of the Atlantic.

Board games like Monopoly offered hours of family entertainment. Although designed during World War II, Cluedo (marketed as Clue in the US) was not yet commercially available but would soon become a household favorite. Model building gained popularity as enthusiasts crafted replicas of wartime trains, planes, and ships. Hornby train sets in the UK allowed hobbyists to create intricate layouts, reflecting a fascination with precision. Other hobbies like knitting and scrapbooking thrived as extensions of wartime skills and thrift.

A vintage 1945 Monopoly set

The first US edition of Clue (marketed as Cluedo) in 1949

Community activities provided spaces for connection and celebration. Local centers hosted dances, amateur theater productions, and musical

1945

performances, helping people reconnect after years of separation. Pubs and cafes in the UK thrived as social hubs, often featuring live music. Festivals and fairs, revived after wartime suspensions, brought joy and community spirit back to towns and villages.

Hornby R3299 1945 "Going Home" Train Pack

Books and magazines offered solace and intellectual engagement. Public libraries experienced a surge in visitors, reflecting a hunger for knowledge and escape. Penguin Books in the UK made literature more accessible with affordable paperbacks, supporting a literate public eager to understand a changing world.

"The Feathers" pub on VE Day in London

In 1945, recreational activities reflected a world eager to rebuild and rediscover joy. From lively dance halls and radio comedies to the tactile pleasures of model building and board games, leisure pursuits provided comfort and connection, helping people recover from war and look toward the future with hope.

Oak Ridge Public Library, 1945

Chapter VI: Births & Deaths 1945

Births (onthisday.com)

January 3 – Stephen Stills: American Singer-Songwriter

January 7 – Raila Odinga: Kenyan Politician

January 10 – Rod Stewart: British Singer-Songwriter

January 10 – Gunther von Hagens: German Anatomist

January 15 – Princess Michael of Kent: Member of the British Royal Family

January 17 – Javed Akhtar: Indian Lyricist and Poet

January 20 – Eric Stewart: English Musician and Producer

January 21 – Martin Shaw: British Actor

January 29 – Tom Selleck: American Actor

February 6 – Bob Marley: Jamaican Reggae Musician

February 9 – Mia Farrow: American Actress

March 8 – Micky Dolenz: American Actor and Musician

1945

March 28 – Rodrigo Duterte: Filipino Politician

March 30 – Eric Clapton: English Guitarist and Singer

April 14 – Ritchie Blackmore: English Guitarist

May 6 – Bob Seger: American Singer-Songwriter

May 19 – Pete Townshend: English Guitarist and Songwriter

May 24 – Priscilla Presley: American Actress

June 19 – Aung San Suu Kyi: Burmese Politician

June 20 – Anne Murray: Canadian Singer

July 1 – Debbie Harry: American Singer

July 26 – Helen Mirren: British Actress

August 14 – Steve Martin: American Actor and Comedian

August 24 – Vince McMahon: American Wrestling Executive

August 31 – Van Morrison: Irish Singer-Songwriter

September 10 – José Feliciano: Puerto Rican Guitarist

September 17 – Phil Jackson: American Basketball Coach

September 26 – Bryan Ferry: English Singer

October 2 – Don McLean: American Singer-Songwriter

October 19 – John Lithgow: American Actor

October 26 – Jaclyn Smith: American Actress

October 30 – Henry Winkler: American Actor

November 12 – Neil Young: Canadian Singer-Songwriter

November 21 – Goldie Hawn: American Actress

December 1 – Bette Midler: American Singer and Actress

December 24 – Lemmy Kilmister: British Musician

Deaths (onthisday.com)

January 2 – Vit Nejedlý: Czech Composer

January 2 – Bertram Ramsay: British Admiral

January 3 – Edgar Cayce: American Psychic

February 1 – Prince Kiril of Bulgaria: Bulgarian Royalty

February 3 – Roland Freisler: German Judge

February 5 – Violette Szabo: British-French SOE Agent

1945

February 6 – Robert Brasillach: French Writer

February 13 – Maria Orosa: Filipino Scientist

February 19 – John Basilone: American War Hero

February 21 – Eric Liddell: Scottish Olympic Athlete

April 9 – Dietrich Bonhoeffer: German Theologian

April 12 – Franklin D. Roosevelt: 32nd U.S. President

April 18 – Ernie Pyle: American Journalist

April 28 – Benito Mussolini: Italian Dictator

April 30 – Adolf Hitler: German Dictator

May 1 – Joseph Goebbels: German Propaganda Minister

May 23 – Heinrich Himmler: German SS Leader

August 6 – Richard Bong: American Fighter Pilot

August 10 – Robert Goddard: American Rocket Pioneer

August 18 – Subhas Chandra Bose: Indian Nationalist Leader

September 15 – Anton Webern: Austrian Composer

December 21 – George S. Patton: American General

Chapter VII: Statistics 1945

GDP

- U.S. GDP 1945 – $223.0 billion (measuringworth.com)
- U.S. GDP 2023 – $27.36 trillion (worldbank.org)
- U.K. GDP 1945 – $26.6 billion (measuringworth.com)
- U.K. GDP 2023 – $3.34 trillion (worldbank.org)

Inflation

- U.S. Inflation 1945 – 2.3% (inflationdata.com)
- U.S. Inflation 2023 – 4.1% (worldbank.org)
- U.K. Inflation 1945 – 3.2% (inflationdata.com)
- U.K. Inflation 2023 – 6.8% (worldbank.org)

Population

- U.S. Population 1945 – 139.9 million (census.gov)
- U.S. Population 2023 – 334.9 million (worldbank.org)
- U.K. Population 1945 – 49.2 million (ons.gov.uk)
- U.K. Population 2023 – 68.35 million (worldbank.org)

Life Expectancy at Birth

- U.S. Life Expectancy at Birth 1945 – 65.9 years (cdc.gov)
- U.S. Life Expectancy at Birth 2022 – 77.0 years (worldbank.org)
- U.K. Life Expectancy at Birth 1945 – 66.3 years (ons.gov.uk)
- U.K. Life Expectancy at Birth 2022 – 82.0 years (worldbank.org)

Annual Working Hours Per Worker

- U.S. Annual Working Hours Per Worker 1945 – 2,100 hours (ourworldindata.org)

- ★ U.S. Annual Working Hours Per Worker 2017 – 1,557 hours (ourworldindata.org)
- ★ U.K. Annual Working Hours Per Worker 1945 – 2,300 hours (ourworldindata.org)
- ★ U.K. Annual Working Hours Per Worker 2017 – 1,670 hours (ourworldindata.org)

Unemployment Rate

- ★ U.S. Unemployment Rate 1945 – 1.9% (bls.gov)
- ★ U.S. Unemployment Rate 2023 – 3.6% (worldbank.org)
- ★ U.K. Unemployment Rate 1945 – 1.6% (ons.gov.uk)
- ★ U.K. Unemployment Rate 2023 – 4.0% (ons.gov.uk)

Tax Revenue (% of GDP)

- ★ U.S. Tax Revenue (% of GDP) 1945 – 20.4% (taxpolicycenter.org)
- ★ U.S. Tax Revenue (% of GDP) 2022 – 12.2% (worldbank.org)
- ★ U.K. Tax Revenue (% of GDP) 1945 – 36.8% (ifs.org.uk)
- ★ U.K. Tax Revenue (% of GDP) 2022 – 27.3% (worldbank.org)

Prison Population

- ★ U.S. Prison Population 1945 – 133,649 inmates (bjs.gov)
- ★ U.S. Prison Population 2021 – 1,230,100 inmates (bjs.ojp.gov)
- ★ U.K. Prison Population 1945 – 15,000 inmates (prisonreformtrust.org.uk)
- ★ U.K. Prison Population 2023 – 97,700 inmates (parliament.uk)

Average Cost of a New House

- ★ U.S. Average Cost of a New House 1945 – $4,600 (census.gov)
- ★ U.S. Average Cost of a New House 2023 – $495,100 (dqydj.com)
- ★ U.K. Average Cost of a New House 1945 – £1,200 (nationwide.co.uk)
- ★ U.K. Average Cost of a New House 2023 – £290,000 (ons.gov.uk)

Average Income per Year

- ★ U.S. Average Income per Year 1945 – $2,400 (census.gov)
- ★ U.S. Average Income per Year 2023 – $106,400 (multpl.com)
- ★ U.K. Average Income per Year 1945 – £300 annually (ons.gov.uk)
- ★ U.K. Average Income per Year 2023 – £34,963 (statista.com)

U.S. Cost of Living

The $100 from 1945 has grown to about $1,753.69 today, up $1,653.69 over 79 years due to an average yearly inflation of 3.69%, resulting in a 1,653.69% total price hike (in2013dollars.com).

U.K. Cost of Living

Today's £5,408.92 mirrors the purchasing power of £100 in 1945, showing a £5,308.92 hike over 79 years. The pound's yearly inflation rate averaged 5.18% during this period, leading to a 5,308.92% total price rise (in2013dollars.com).

Cost Of Things

United States

- ★ Men's jacket, Sheepskin Mackinaw: $22.50 (mclib.info)
- ★ Men's suits: $27.95 - $44.95 (mclib.info)
- ★ Women's skirts: $2.98 - $5.98 (mclib.info)
- ★ Women's dress shoes, patent leather pumps: $8.95 (mclib.info)
- ★ Hats, women's "Beau catchers": $4.00 (mclib.info)
- ★ Fresh eggs (1 dozen): $0.58 (stacker.com)
- ★ White bread (1 pound): $0.09 (stacker.com)
- ★ Sliced bacon (1 pound): $0.41 (stacker.com)
- ★ Round steak (1 pound): $0.41 (stacker.com)

- ★ Potatoes (10 pounds): $0.49 (stacker.com)
- ★ Tomatoes (Number 2 can): $0.10 (mclib.info)
- ★ Peanut butter, Skippy (1 lb jar): $0.33 (mclib.info)
- ★ Tea, Ehlers, bags (48 count box): $0.41 (mclib.info)
- ★ Jelly, grape, Ann Page (1 lb jar): $0.20 (mclib.info)
- ★ Coffee, Sanka, decaffeinated (1 lb jar): $0.36 (mclib.info)
- ★ Cereal, Kellogg's Corn Flakes (6 oz package): $0.05 (mclib.info)
- ★ Soup, tomato, Campbell's (3 cans): $0.25 (mclib.info)

United Kingdom (retrowow.co.uk)
- ★ Gallon of petrol: 1s 6d (nationalarchives.gov.uk)
- ★ Pint of beer: 1s 2d (northumberlandgazette.co.uk)
- ★ 20 cigarettes: 2s 4d (northumberlandgazette.co.uk)
- ★ Loaf of bread (white, unwrapped): 4½d (northumberlandgazette.co.uk)
- ★ Pint of milk: 4d (northumberlandgazette.co.uk)
- ★ Eggs (1 dozen): 3s 8d (northumberlandgazette.co.uk)
- ★ Cheddar cheese (1 lb): 1s 8d (northumberlandgazette.co.uk)
- ★ Butter (½ lb): 1s 2d (northumberlandgazette.co.uk)
- ★ Eating apples (1 lb): 8d (northumberlandgazette.co.uk)
- ★ Potatoes (1 lb): 2d (northumberlandgazette.co.uk)
- ★ Onions (1 lb): 3½d (northumberlandgazette.co.uk)
- ★ Oranges (1 lb): 7d (northumberlandgazette.co.uk)
- ★ Penguin chocolate bar: 2d (northumberlandgazette.co.uk)
- ★ Murphy A104 tabletop radio: £31 11s 1d (theanswerbank.co.uk)
- ★ Qualcast Panther push lawn mower: £5 10s (nationalarchives.gov.uk)
- ★ Three Nuns pipe tobacco (1 oz): 2s 7d (theanswerbank.co.uk)

Chapter VIII: Iconic Advertisements of 1945

Campbell's Vegetable Soup

General Electric Lamps

Kellogg's All-Bran

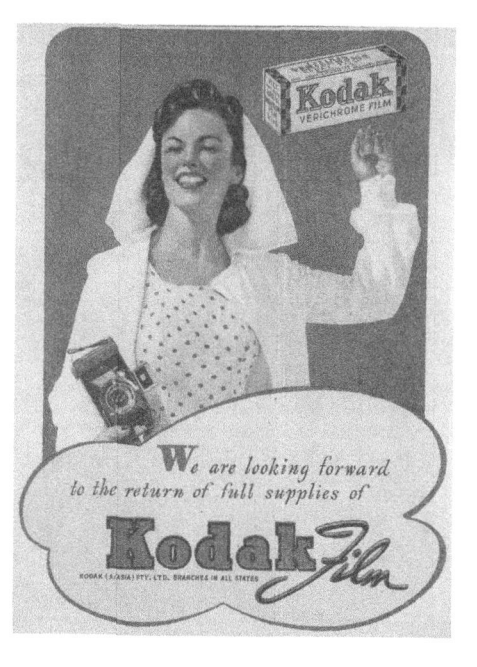

Kodak Verichrome Film

1945

Old St. Croix Rum

Chesterfield

Nescafé

Pepsodent

98

1945

Milky Way Candy Bars

Firestone DeLuxe Champion Tires

Blatz Beer

Philip Morris Pipe Tobacco

1945

Palmolive

Plymouth

Armour Star Treet: Canned Lunch Meat

The Hoover Company

1945

Kool-Aid

Lucky Strike

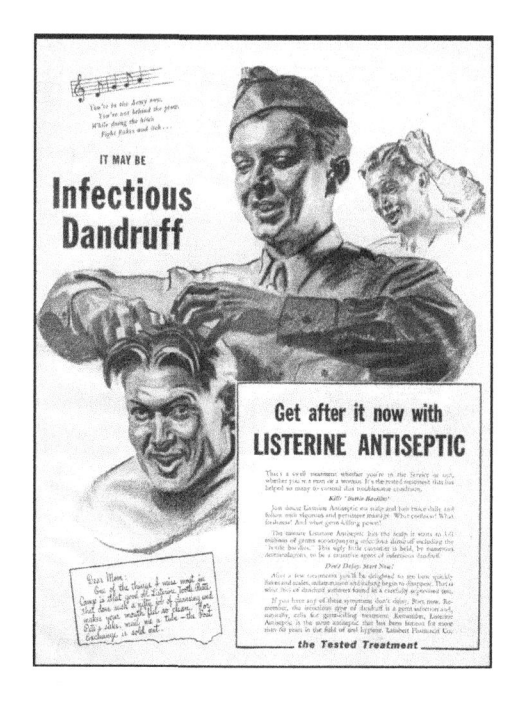

Listerine Antiseptic

Ford

101

1945

7-Up

Pan American World Airways

Nabisco: Ritz Crackers

General Electric FM Radio featuring Carmen Miranda

1945

Riondo: Distilled Puerto Rican Rum

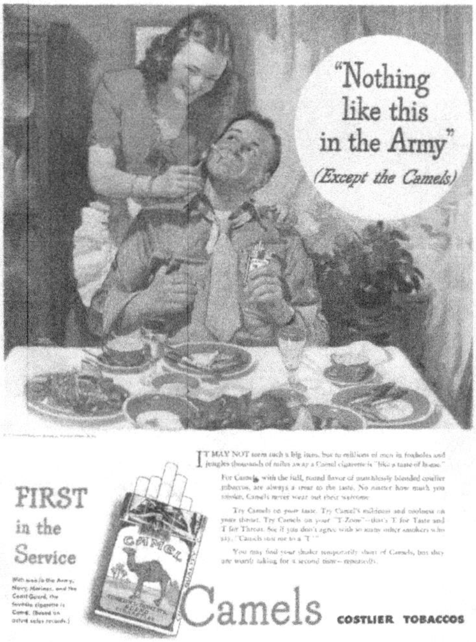

Camels

Procter & Gamble: Duz

Coca-Cola

U.S. Government 1945 War Bonds

1945 Buick Ad Featuring a 1942 Model
(as civilian car production nearly halted during the war years)

I have a gift for you!

Dear reader, thank you so much for reading my book!

To make this book more (much more!) affordable, all images are in black and white, but I've created a special gift for you!

You can now have access, for FREE, to the PDF version of this book with the original images!

Keep in mind that some are originally black and white, but some are colored.

I hope you enjoy it!

Download it here:

bit.ly/4fuinqu

Or Scan this QR Code:

I have a favor to ask you!

I deeply hope you've enjoyed reading this book and felt transported right into 1945!

I loved researching it, organizing it, and writing it, knowing that it would make your day a little brighter.

If you've enjoyed it too, I would be extremely grateful if you took just a few minutes to leave a positive customer review and share it with your friends.

As an unknown author, that makes all the difference and gives me the extra energy I need to keep researching, writing, and bringing joy to all my readers. Thank you!

Best regards,
Clark P. Ridley

Please leave a positive book review here:

https://amzn.to/49Q4BNW

Or Scan this QR Code:

Discover Other Books in this Collection!